The Li ... ook of Time and Place

Ideas for helping children in the Foundation Stage to develop a Sense of Time and Place

Written by
Linda Thornton and Pat Brunton

Illustrations by Martha Hardy

Little Books with **BIG** ideas®

The Little Book of Time & Place
ISBN 1 904187 95 1

©Featherstone Education Ltd, 2004
Text © Pat Brunton & Linda Thornton, 2004
Illustrations © Martha Hardy, 2004

Series Editor, Sally Featherstone

First published in the UK, June 2004

'Little Books' is a trade mark of Featherstone Education Ltd

Published in the United Kingdom by
Featherstone Education Ltd
44 - 46 High Street
Husbands Bosworth
Leicestershire
LE17 6LP

Printed in the UK on paper produced in the European Union from managed, sustainable forests

Contents

Introduction

The Little Book of Time and Place focuses on two aspects of the Foundation Stage curriculum area of Knowledge and Understanding of the World, a sense of time and a sense of place. The activities also provide many opportunities for children to develop their skills of communication, to broaden their experience of different cultures and beliefs and to develop positive dispositions and attitudes to learning.

Throughout the daily life of your setting there will be many opportunities to broaden children's understanding of place and time. When you are talking with individuals or with groups of children you will be able to reflect with them and recollect things which have happened.

Plan these 'memories' into your daily routines to give children lots of experience of 'now' and 'the past', 'here' and 'other places'. The past in this context could be 'a long time ago', or just yesterday. 'Other places' could be the outdoor area of your setting, places in the local environment or other countries. The activities in this book are designed to support children's day to day experiences by providing specific ideas and activities to develop their understanding of time and place.

Individual children's awareness of 'a sense of time' will vary. Some children join your setting with little apparent awareness of the past while others may already have been exposed to a strong oral tradition of family history. The same will apply to the children's understanding of places; some children's experiences will be within their own environment, whilst others will have travelled widely within the U.K. and beyond.

The Little Book of Time and Place looks at the areas of learning which link with history and geography at Key Stage 1.

A Sense of Time (History)

The study of the passing of time (History) has three aspects:
* change over time,
* accounts of life in the past and
* investigating the traces of the past which remain.

In the Foundation Stage, understanding change over time is about measuring the passing of time, sequencing events in chronological order and being aware of similarities and differences between the past and the present.

Accounts of life in the past will have been written by different people, from different perspectives. Children can be helped to appreciate this by comparing their memories of a recent event with those of their friends. Through stories and imaginative play children in the Foundation Stage they will also have the opportunity to identify with people and events in the past.

Investigating traces of the past happens through hearing accounts and stories, looking at photographs and pictures, visiting old buildings and handling artefacts from the past.

A Sense of Place (Geography)

Geography is the study of:
* places,
* people and
* environments.

In the Foundation Stage children will become increasingly aware of their own surroundings, recognising where things are and why they are there. Some children will be familiar with features of other localities and will begin to recognise similarities and differences between places.

Learning about people will help children to understand their place in the world and to consider others. They will begin to have a greater awareness of cultural differences and to develop ideas of citizenship. Developing a respect for the environment and thinking about how people affect it, helps to foster the children's sense of wonder about the world around them.

How the book works

The activities are grouped into four themes relating to children's experiences. They are:
* My Family
* With my Friends
* Where I Live and
* Journeys.

The sections are colour coded for ease of reference.

The 'Focus' title for each activity focuses on one aspect of A sense of time or a sense of place selected for the book.

'Making connections' shows how you could link activities together to build on one another. For example, **'Every day'** is a starting point for **'Places I like'** and **'Going shopping'** links with **'What we like to eat'**.

'Key words' are included to extend children's vocabulary for talking and thinking about time and place

'Getting started' provides ideas for resources and discussions to introduce the main activity.

'Exploring time and place' describes in detail an exploration related to the theme of the activity.

'More ideas' suggests other activities to reinforce, expand or extend children's understanding of time and place.

The Background Information section you will find a list of children's books which you could use as starting points.
It also contains a selection of songs and rhymes, and some contacts and web sites for further information.

6

What are they learning?

Remember

Exploring time and place can:

! Give the children multi sensory experiences and encourage them to think about the memories which these prompt.

! Make full use of the outdoor environment by increasing children's awareness of the indoors and the outdoors and by moving some indoor activities outside.

! Involve families in the life of the setting, and in their children's learning.

! Value visitors, visits and opportunities to recollect and reminisce.

! Foster a caring attitude towards the environment, both in the setting and in the wider world.

! Introduce children and their families to the notion of citizenship.

! Develop cultural awareness and understanding.

! Create an exciting and purposeful use for the wheeled toys in your setting!

Developing skills, dispositions and attitudes

Exploring a sense of time and place will help to develop a range of historical and geographical skills. These include:

⚥ social skills of cooperation, negotiation, leadership, following instructions, understanding rules and personal safety.

⚥ communication skills including speaking, listening, discussing, questioning, referencing and recording.

⚥ practical skills including using all the senses, observation, construction and measuring time and distance.

⚥ reasoning and thinking skills including questioning, speculating and inferring, sequencing, noticing similarities and differences, making links, reflecting and reminiscing.

To help children master the range of skills they need there is also range of behaviours, or positive dispositions which you can help to foster. These include curiosity and imagination, empathy with and valuing others and critical reflection.

Emotional health warning!

Encouraging children and adults to share their memories and their personal experiences can involve strong emotions and feelings. Be aware of, and sensitive to this.

Linking the activities to the Curriculum

The activities in the The Little Book of Time and Place, and the way in which they support the development of children as young historians and geographers, will support the Early Learning Goals for:

Knowledge and Understanding of the World - **A sense of place**

Observe, find out and identify features in the place they live and the natural world.
Find out about their environment, and talk about those features they like and dislike.

Knowledge and Understanding of the World - **A sense of time**

Identify simple features and significant personal events
Find out about the past and present events in their own lives, and in those of family members and other people they know.

Knowledge and Understanding of the World - **Exploration and investigation**

Investigate objects and materials by using all of their senses as appropriate.
Find out, and identify, some features of living things, objects, and events they observe.
Look closely at similarities, differences, patterns and change.
Ask questions about why things happen and how things work.

Knowledge and Understanding of the World - Designing and making skills

Build and construct with a wide range of objects, selecting appropriate resources and adapting their work where necessary. Select the tools and techniques they need to shape, assemble and join the materials they are making.

Knowledge and Understanding of the World - ICT

Find out and identify the uses of everyday technology and use information and communication technology to support their learning.

Personal, Social and Emotional Development - Dispositions and attitudes

Be confident to try new activities, initiate ideas and speak in a familiar group.
Maintain attention, concentrate, and sit quietly when appropriate.
Continue to be interested, excited and motivated to learn.

Personal, Social and Emotional Development - Social and emotional development

Communicate freely about home and community.
Work as part of a group, taking turns and sharing fairly,
Understand that there need to be agreed values and codes of behaviour for groups of people, including adults and children, to work together harmoniously.

Creative Development - Responding to experiences, expressing & communicating ideas

Respond in a variety of ways to what they see, hear, smell, touch and feel.
Express experiences and ideas through role play.

Communication, language and literacy - Language for communication

Interact with others, negotiating plans and activities and taking turns in conversations.
Sustain active listening, responding to what they have heard by relevant comments, questions or actions.
Extend their vocabulary, exploring the meanings and sounds of new words.

Communication, language and literacy - **Language for thinking**

Use talk to organise, sequence and clarifying thinking, ideas, feelings and events.

Mathematical development - **Shape, space and measures**

Use everyday words to describe position.
Use developing mathematical ideas and methods to solve practical problems.

Physical development - **Using equipment, tools and materials**

Use a range of small and large equipment.
Handle tools, objects, construction and malleable materials safely and with increasing control.

Contributions to the Foundation Stage Profile

Area of Learning	Scale and statements	
Knowledge and Understanding of the World	KUW	1,2,3,4,5,6,7,8,9.
Personal, Social and Emotional Development	DA	1,3,5,6,7,8,9.
	SD	1,2,3,4,5,6,7,8,9.
	ED	2,4,5,6,7,8,9.
Creative Development	CD	2,3,4,7,8,9.
Communication, Language and Literacy	LCT	1,2,3,6,7,8,9.
	W	6,8.
Mathematical Development	SSM	1,2,3,4,5,6,7,8,9.
Physical Development	PD	1,2,3,5,6,7,9.

A Sense of Time

and Place

Focus: Who we are
Theme: My Family

> 'Who we are' focuses on the child's position within his or her family and community.

Making connections

'Who we are' could link to:
'Everyone's Special Day',
'Keeping in touch',
'Growing up'
and topics on
All about me
Ourselves

Key words

* family
* grandfather
* mother
* grandmother
* father
* older
* sister
* younger
* brother
* first
* cousin
* age

Getting started

☺ Collect a range of resources which show family life – books, magazines, photographs. Include people from several generations

☺ Be sensitive to the many different family structures which exist within your setting and community.

☺ Show cultural diversity by using positive images with which the children can identify.

☺ You could introduce two or three Persona dolls into your setting to model different types of family.

☺ With the whole group talk about family members and their relationships to one another.

☺ You could use your own family to illustrate a 'family time line' of different generations – children, parents, grandparents.

Exploring time and place

1. Encourage families to support their children's learning by providing photographs of a their family members. Remember that some families may not have photographs available - drawings will work just as well.
2. Provide a variety of different types of paper for the children to choose from.
3. Help each child to make a 'zig zag' book which shows their family in sequence – starting with the youngest.
   Some children will want to write about their family members in their book (either by dictating words to you or writing independently themselves).
4. Making the family zig zag time line will give you the opportunity to introduce time related vocabulary such as before, after, older, younger.
5. You could also introduce mathematical vocabulary for ordering numbers – first, second, third.
6. Provide opportunities for the children to talk about their families using the 'zig zag' books they have made.
7. Use your Persona dolls to encourage children to empathise with family situations other than their own.

And another idea......

* Use old photographs of family groups to look at things 'then and now'.
* Some of the children's photographs may show family members in other places – use these for group discussion.
* Make zigzag books of families with one family member on each page (include pets if you like!).

What we like to eat
Theme: My Family

'What we like to eat' looks at food from around the world -where it comes from, how it is prepared and cooked.

Making connections

'What we like to eat' could link with:
'Everyone's Special Day'
'Keeping in touch'
'Going shopping'
'On holiday'
and to topics on
Food or Farming

Key words
* fruit
* vegetable
* like
* dislike
* taste
* cook
* prepare
* special
* favourite
* garden
* farm
* market

Getting started

☺ Start with a discussion with the children about their families' favourite foods.

☺ Have available a range of cookery books with colour illustrations, recipe leaflets from supermarkets and magazines.

☺ Encourage the children to describe different foods – what they look like, what they taste like, how they are cooked and where they are bought.

☺ Talk with the children about where different foods come from – look at pictures of farms, gardens, allotments, crops and fruit trees. It may be possible to arrange a visit to a local farm or allotment.

☺ Buy breads from other cultures for the children to try. Include pitta, ciabatta, chapatti, croissant, soda bread.

Exploring time and place

1. Plan to hold a 'special food day' when you prepare, with the children, (and parents if possible) a range of food with different cultural influences. Try to involve families in the celebration.
2. Decide, with the children, which dishes are going to be made and what you are going to need.
3. Take the opportunity to include children in a shopping expedition to the local market or supermarket.
4. Ask them to tell the other children about their experience – where they went, how they travelled, what they saw and did.
5. Organise groups of children to:
    - help prepare and cook the dishes from around the world,
    - decorate the setting,
    - lay the tables
    - invite the guests.
6. Take photographs to record the whole event to add to a Sense of Time book for your setting. Remember to include children's comments with the photos.

Remember that some children are allergic to certain foods. Check your records to avoid problems.

And another idea......

* Use simple recipes for sequencing events and following instructions. Try some simple pictorial recipes that children can do by themselves.
* Grow mustard and cress, radishes and bean sprouts to eat. Make a daily diary of drawings and photos as they grow.

Things we use
Theme: My Family

'Things we use' compares daily life during the time of the children's grandparents with life today.

Making connections

'Things we use' could link with:
'What we like to eat'
'Games and rhymes'
'Toys'
'A day out'
and topics on
Then and now.

Key words

* now
* then
* past
* same
* different
* today
* grandparent
* child
* old
* new
* aunt
* uncle

Getting started

☺ Gather together a collection of objects that would have been used around the home in the past. Charity shops are a useful source.

☺ These could include kitchen utensils, an old camera, a dial telephone, fire irons, radio, record player, coins and money, jigsaws, children's books.

☺ Talk with the children about the collection of objects, what they were used for and how they compare with what we use today. Talk about how we used to keep warm, do housework and cooking.

☺ Invite one or more grandparents to come in to talk to the children about daily life when they were young -they may bring pictures and photographs to share. Perhaps you will be able to include grandparents who grew up in different parts of the world.

The Little Book of Time & Place

Exploring time and place

1. Set up the role play area as a home environment from the past. For 'In the kitchen' you could have:

wooden clothes horse	wooden dolly pegs and peg bag
shopping bag	doilies
broom and mop	old iron and ironing board
shopping basket	clothes airer

   Clothes:

aprons	high heeled shoes
headscarves	caps, braces
hair ribbons	hair rollers
Fair Isle tank tops	short sleeved shirts and ties

   Games:

hula hoop	skipping ropes, marbles, jacks
bricks and planks	Ludo, dominoes
snakes and ladders	happy families

2. Encourage the children to become involved in imaginative play indoors and out – washing the dolls clothes (including nappies), making dens, playing outdoor games, pushing the doll's pram. Talk with the children about daily life in the past and now.

And another idea......

* Cook with the children using old recipes – jam tarts, rock buns, cup cakes, scones, toffee cakes, fairy cakes, soup or coconut ice.
* The older children will enjoy looking at commemorative mugs, spoons and jigsaws.

Keeping in touch
Theme: My Family

> 'Keeping in touch' focuses on communication between people and places.

Making connections

'Keeping in touch' could link with
'Everyone's Special Day'
'On holiday' or 'In our street'
and links to topics on
Around the world
Communication

Key words

* letter	* telephone	* address	* near
* postcard	* map	* country	* home
* stamp	* globe	* far	* away

Getting started

☺ Gather together a selection of examples of different forms of communication. These could include:

     letters,   e mail,

     cards,   postcards

☺ Talk about how we use telephones and text messages.

☺ Invite the postman or the telephone engineer into your setting to talk about the job they do. This will give you the opportunity to talk about places close by and places far away, and how addresses are used.

☺ Discuss with the children about the importance of families and friends keeping in touch.

☺ Be sensitive to different family circumstances.

Exploring time and place

1. Set up a communication area where you provide:
   - Cards, paper, postcards and other writing materials
   - Stamps and a post box
   - A selection of telephones.

   You may wish to add a globe or a map of the world.

2. Encourage the children to send messages. These could be to:
   - Other children in the group
   - Children in another group or class
   - Family members.

3. Help the children to organise a rota of who will be postman. The postman will be responsible for delivering mail in the setting.

4. You will need to decide how messages to family members are going to be delivered – receiving their replies will cause great excitement in your setting.

5. Think about positioning the communication area near to the door and put the post box outside. You could use the bikes for postal delivery vans, or make a parcel and letter sorting office outside.

6. Try making a speaking tube using funnels and wide plastic tubing for communication between the indoors and the outside.

And another idea......

* Make a collection of post-cards from around the world and look on the globe to find out where they came from.
* Use communication boxes made from shoe boxes to encourage children to exchange messages.
* Find a partner setting or school and exchange letters or e-mails.

Everyone's special day
Theme: My Family

'Everyone's Special Day' will create a resource for children to look back on and remember events and traditions.

Making connections

'Everyone's Special Day' could link with 'Who we are', 'What we like to eat' and 'What are you wearing today?' as well as topics on
Christmas,
Festivals,
Harvest.

Key words

* celebrate
* special
* festival

* party
* wedding
* birthday

* photograph
* remember
* before

* after
* present
* card

Getting started

☺ Encourage the children to bring in photographs of themselves and their families at celebrations in the past- birthdays, weddings, naming ceremonies, New Year festivals and religious celebrations.

☺ Talk to the children about the traditions associated with these celebrations- what happens, what people wear, what they eat.

☺ You will need to make sure that the children are aware of a wide range of celebrations and traditions which reflect different cultures and beliefs.

☺ You could show the children clothes, artefacts and music which link to different celebrations.

☺ You will need to make sure that the children are aware of a wide range of celebrations and traditions which reflect different cultures and beliefs.

Exploring time and place

1. Choose, or make, a large book to record the celebrations in the children's photographs. The book could be called 'Everyone's Special Day.' Make sure you include the staff's special days too.
2. Work with each child to produce a page in the book. This could include:

   - a photograph,
   - mark making,
   - a transcript of the child's description of their special day,
   - a drawing or painting,
   - word processing.

3. When the book is finished put it in the book corner for all to read.
4. The children will use the book to remember their own special occasions and to share in the experiences of others.
5. Offer family members the opportunity to visit your setting to look at 'Everyone's Special Day' and to reminisce with their children.
6. Keep the big book to use as a resource in the future.

Note: Ask parents if you can keep copies of the photos they bring as a permanent resource for the setting.

And another idea......

* Provide opportunities for the children to make their own cards and invitations from simple materials.
* Children could use simple ICT programs to make letters and invitations.
* Use the resources of the role play area to re-enact special days.

Every day

Theme: With my friends

'Everyday' focuses on children's daily routines, sequencing events and recognising familiar places.

Making connections

'Everyday' could link with
'What are you wearing today?'
'Places I like',
and topics on
Our setting or school,
Time.

Key words	* first	* after	* beginning	* day
	* then	* start	* end	* like
	* before	* finish	* time	* dislike

Getting started

☺ Gather together any posters, notices or timetables you have in the setting which set out the pattern of the day.

☺ Talk with the children about the pattern of the day and discuss different times of the day which have special significance for them. These might range from 'Saying goodbye',' Playing my favourite game,' ' Playing outside', 'Snack time' or 'Story time'.

☺ With some of the children, make an object time line of familiar things relating to each activity -a mug for snack time, an apron for cooking, a coat for going outside, a book for story time etc. put them in time order.

☺ Use these objects each day to help children recall things that have happened and predict what comes next.

Exploring time and place

1. Take small groups of children on a walk around your setting and talk with them about the different activities which happen in different areas. Remember to include the entrance area, the different areas outside the setting, the office area and any cooking or eating areas you have.

2. Talk with the children about the activities which happen in different areas and be prepared to record or note down the comments they make and the conversations they have.

3. Help the children to take photographs of the different areas and activities and provide resources for them to draw pictures and paintings of activities which particularly interest them.

4. Collect the pictures, drawings, photos and comments, and help the children to sequence them into a time line which demonstrates the activities of the setting during a typical session.

5. Agree a place to display this – ideally at child height in the entrance or cloakroom area where it will be easily visible to children, families and visitors.

6. Encourage the children to share the time line with their families.

And another idea......

* Draw some simple pictures of activities (or use photos). Stick a bit of Velcro on the back of each, and put the other strip of the Velcro on a pinboard or a piece of sturdy card. Use this to make a time line for each day, with significant events in time order.

* Make simple zigzag books of familiar events in order.

What are you wearing today?

Theme: With my friends

'What are you wearing today?' looks at clothes you could wear in different places, and at different times of day.

Making connections

'What are you wearing today?' could link with
'Every day', 'On holiday'
'In our street'
and topics on
Clothes,
Keeping safe.

Key words

* clothes
* warm
* dry
* clean
* safe
* place
* rules
* signs
* poster
* indoors
* outdoors
* protect

Getting started

☺ Set up a washing line with a variety of clothing pegged on to it. Include aprons, rainwear, outdoor protective clothing, wellington boots, sun hats, safety goggles, sweatshirt, coats, pyjamas, reflective strip or waistcoat, baby clothes, night wear.

☺ Talk about the different types of clothing, what they are for, who wears them and when they would be worn.

☺ Draw attention to keeping warm, staying dry and clean and being safe.

☺ You might want to take the opportunity to think about wearing different clothing at different times of the day or different seasons. Look back at the photographs of babies and toddlers to see what they are wearing.

Exploring time and place

1. Discuss with the children why we need to wear protective clothing and where it could be worn in the setting. For example: aprons or shirts in the painting area, protective goggles at the workbench, waterproofs or sunhats when playing outdoors, aprons or napkins at the snack table.
2. Talk to the children about why we have rules about personal safety. Involve them in deciding what is worn where in your setting. How will everyone know the rules? Discuss different ways of getting the information across to everyone in the setting (notices, labels, etc.).
3. Help the children to produce ideas for posters, signs or instructions for each of the areas of your setting. These could include photos, paintings, models, simple notices and symbols.
3. Help the children to position the signs in the best places in the setting. This will promote a discussion in itself.
3. After a week talk to the children about how successful you all feel their signs and posters have been – include the staff views. Do you have to move some, or say something different, or make them more noticeable?

And another idea......

* Look at hats from around the world. Talk to the children about who would wear them, and why.
* Compare clothes you would wear in hot and cold places, inside and outside, during the day and at night. This is an opportunity to investigate materials used around the world in different seasons, weathers and climates.

Toys
Theme: With my friends

'Toys' focuses on the difference between toys then and now and the importance of valuing and respecting precious things.

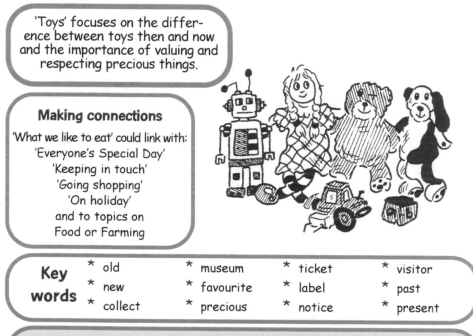

Making connections

'What we like to eat' could link with:
'Everyone's Special Day'
'Keeping in touch'
'Going shopping'
'On holiday'
and to topics on
Food or Farming

Key words

* old	* museum	* ticket	* visitor
* new	* favourite	* label	* past
* collect	* precious	* notice	* present

Getting started

☺ Read the children the story 'Old Bear' by Jane Hissey. Talk about the toys in the story and the children's favourite toys in the home or in the setting. Discuss what they look like, what they are made of, how they work and what they do.

☺ Find ways of drawing the children's attention to the differences between old and new toys. If possible arrange a visit to a local museum which has a section on toys.

☺ Look at how collections of toys are displayed, how they are described, and how they are looked after. Some museums or libraries operate a lending service.

☺ You may decide to build up your own collection of old toys from donations and charity shops. Make sure that all these toys are clean and safe for the children to handle.

Exploring time and place

1. Involve the children and families in setting up a toy museum. Decide with the children where the museum will be – a place where the toys are accessible but safe.
2. Ask older family members to lend an old toy for your collection. You will need to find out a little about each of the toys - name, age, who it belongs and why it is special. Some toy owners may be willing to visit the setting to talk about their memories of and adventures with their toys.
3. Help the children to label and display the toys in their museum. This is an opportunity to produce posters, guidebooks, information leaflets and entrance tickets in the mark making area. Provide real examples of museum information for the children to look at. Invite families and friends in to visit the museum.
4. A selection of books on old toys will encourage the children to begin to use reference material to find out more them.
5. Choose a day when the children bring in their own favourites toy. Spend time talking about the toys and comparing them with those in the museum collection.

And another idea......

* Use a toy collection to look at the different ways in which toys move – push and pull, stretch, clockwork, batteries, wind, water.
* Collect some examples of toys and dolls from around the world and look at materials used in toy making, and national dress.

Try charity shops for toys made from recycled materials such as tin cans, cogs, tyres etc.

Games and rhymes
Theme: With my friends

'Games and Rhymes' looks at playing group games out of doors in the past and the present.

Making connections

'Games and rhymes' could link with
'Things we use',
'A Day Out'
and topics on
The Victorians
Games and Pastimes.

Key words	* game	* past	* history	* circle
	* rhyme	* time	* turn	* ring
	* song	* long ago	* line	* clap

Getting started

☺ Twenty or thirty years ago children played many different dancing and singing games in small and large groups, out of doors and on special occasions such as parties.

☺ Many of the traditional group and circle games had a historic background, with reference to people and events, for example 'The Grand Old Duke of York', and 'Ring-a –Roses' which is about the plague in England. Many of these rhymes and games have a local version which children will enjoy finding out about.

☺ Have available a selection of Nursery Rhyme and song books and tapes for the children to look at. There are many examples of traditional rhymes, songs and games in:

The Little Book of Nursery Rhymes, The Little Book of Maths Songs and Games, The Little Book of Playground Games.

Exploring time and place

1. During singing sessions with the children in your setting, introduce some nursery rhymes and songs which have a historic background. Older children will like to hear about what the words.
2. Take the children outdoors to play some of these circle games:
   - ⚙ 'The Grand Old Duke of York'
   - ⚙ 'Ring-a – roses'
   - ⚙ 'Oranges and Lemons'
   - ⚙ 'The Big Ship Sails through the Alley O'.
   - ⚙ 'Do you know the muffin man?'
3. All these games are rooted in the past and will give a starting point to talk about events which happened long ago.
4. You can find the words and actions for these games at the end of the book, in the Background Information section.
3. You may find that staff and family members know other circle games which are local to your area or which are played in other parts of the world. Invite them to join in!
3. Try some other games from the past such as hopscotch, marbles, Jacks (sometimes called Snobs, Fivestones, Dabstones), spinning tops, skipping games, even conkers!

And another idea......

* Use the singing game 'There was a Princess Long Ago' or the nursery rhyme 'London Bridge is Falling Down' to stimulate castle and bridge building in the construction area.
* Sing action songs such as 'Wind the Bobbin' and 'Oats and Beans' which are related to work in the past.

Growing up
Theme: With my friends

'Growing up' focuses on sequencing the different stages of growth and development.

Making connections

'Growing up' could link with 'Who we are', 'Everyone's Special Day', and topics on :
All About Me,
My family.

Key words

* baby
* toddler
* child
* teenager
* adult
* grown up
* younger
* older
* same
* different
* guess
* order

Getting started

☺ Collect a wide range of pictures, photographs and illustrations of babies, children and families.

☺ Talk with the children about how we recognise people - their features, such as shape of face, colour of eyes and hair, size.

☺ Draw their attention to what babies and toddlers are able and not able to do.

☺ Play a game of 'Guess who?'. One person describes another person without naming them. The rest of the group have to try and guess who it is. This helps children to focus more closely on individual features.

☺ Provide children with mirrors so they can look at themselves and describe their own features. Encourage them to look at their reflections and make drawings and pictures of themselves.

Exploring time and place

1. Ask the parents to send in a photograph of their child when they were a baby or a toddler. Provide them with an envelope to put it in.
2. Explain that this is a secret as it is going to be used as part of a quiz. Keeping things secret will be a challenge for everyone!
3. Make a display of the photographs. Remember to include photos of staff members.
4. Work with small groups (2 or 3 at a time) to talk about the photos so that they can work on recognising their friends as babies or toddlers. This will provide an opportunity to talk about different stages of growing up. You might be able to draw simple historical comparisons using the staff photographs – clothes, hairstyles, toys.
5. When everyone has had a look at the photographs, have a whole group discussion about the photos and the different stages of development they show. You might need to provide additional pictures of babies and young children to help the sequence.
6. Ask the children to arrange the photographs in order. This could lead to some children making a sequenced photo album of themselves and their friends and families.

And another idea......

* Many children may have pets. Talk about animals and their young.
* Provide books, resources and models of life cycles of animals and plants.
* Try a butterfly box, an ant farm or even an incubator with some chicken or duck eggs.
* Take them to a farm park or children's zoo.

Places I like
Theme: Where I live

'Places I like' helps children to investigate the environment with all their senses, and to say what they like and dislike.

Making connections

'Places I like' could link with 'Everyday', 'Moving house' or 'What are you wearing today?' and to topics on Our setting/school, Using our senses.

Key words

* place
* inside
* outside
* look
* smell
* sound
* feel
* taste
* like
* dislike
* change
* think

Getting started

☺ Take time to find out how the children feel about the environment (the setting) you share. Listen carefully to the children and be prepared to make changes in response to what they say.

☺ A 'time line of the day' (as in the project 'Everyday') makes a good starting point for this activity.

☺ Gather together photographs of different areas of your setting and any maps or plans the children have made. Discuss these with the children. Talk about inside and outside, and help them to recall earlier comments and observations, including their likes and dislikes.

☺ Talk about the different ways we experience our surroundings – what they look like, what they smell like, what they sound like and what they feel like.

☺ Play games which help them focus on using all their senses.

Exploring time and place

1. Working with small groups of children, go on a tour of your setting, inside and out. Help the children to experience each area , not just what it looks like, but how it sounds and smells and feels as well.
2. Encourage the children to express their opinions and preferences and be record some of these – taking notes or using a tape recorder.
3. Provide a disposable (or digital) camera so the children can take their own photographs of the areas they like and dislike.
4. Provide opportunities for small groups to share their comments and observations with the rest of the children. Use open questions to help children to express their ideas and share their opinions and views.
5. Ask the children to make drawings, pictures and models to accompany their comments and ideas.
6. Assemble these into a display which gives an unique 'child's eye view' of your setting.
7. Talk about your own likes and dislikes. Some adults like being outside, others don't! Some like construction, others the role play area. Let the children hear your comments, likes and dislikes.
8. Now move on to a discussion about how you could change some of the areas and what effect this would have on everyone.

And another idea......

* Use photographs of the children showing different emotions and expressions to help develop their sensitivity to others needs.
* Explore shape and pattern in the environment using the photographs the children have taken
* Invite parents and carers in to see the Child's Eye View Exhibition'.

Our house
Theme: Where I live

'Our house' is about the different places and types of houses which people live in.

Making connections

'Our house' could link with:
'In our street', 'Moving house'
'Building a house', and topics on
Where we live, Homes, In the town.

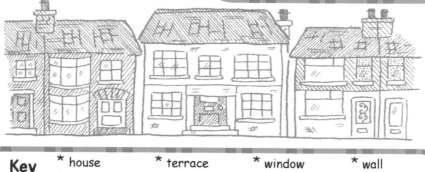

Key words

* house	* terrace	* window	* wall
* flat	* caravan	* roof	* number
* bungalow	* door	* chimney	* name

Getting started

☺ Gather together a selection of pictures of houses from books, magazines, estate agent's literature.

☺ Don't forget to include a wide variety of different homes including caravans. You could provide photos of familiar houses close to the setting.

☺ Remember to use the correct vocabulary to describe different types of house and to make children aware of the many different types which exist.

☺ Talk about the features which may be common to different houses – doors, windows, roofs, chimneys, bricks and walls.

☺ If you have a suitable dolls' house you could use it to talk about the different parts which make up the house.

Exploring time and place

1. Go for a walk in the local neighbourhood. Provide the children with clipboards and encourage them to draw the different types of houses they see.
2. Let them take some photographs to accompany their drawings.
3. When you get back tot he setting, talk about the houses you have seen and the drawings and photos the children have made.
4. Ask the children to describe the house they live in. With open questioning and prompting you will be able to help them recall some of the detail of where they live.
5. Each child can then draw a picture of their own house. This is a good opportunity for children use fine pens and pencils to produce more detailed drawings. Try offering fine black marker pens, no colour.
6. Use the children's pictures and drawings to construct a 2D street collage.
7. The street can then be recreated in 3D using small scale construction, cardboard boxes or clay.
8. You can use the street to develop vocabulary relating to position, size, distance, pattern and materials.

And another idea......

* Take opportunities to talk about the significance of house numbers, both on the walk and in constructing the imaginary street.
* Some children could draw a plan of the walk. This can be enlarged and can include the photographs and drawings made by other children.

Moving house
Theme: Where I live

'Moving house' is about understanding the connections between places and the notion of living somewhere different.

Making connections

'Moving house' could link with 'Everyday', 'In our street' 'Building a House', 'Keeping in touch' and with topics on On the Move, Families.

Key words

* move
* house
* removal
* place
* lift
* plan
* pack
* safe
* load
* indoors
* outdoors
* van

Getting started

☺ Use one of these books to talk about moving house, and all the different feelings and stages involved.
'The Berenstain Bear's Moving Day'; 'Moving House' – Usborne First Experiences, 'Moving Molly' - Red Fox

☺ You could invite a new parent or family member to talk to the children about their experiences when moving house.

☺ Alternatively you could invite a member of staff from a removal firm to come in and talk about their job.

☺ Talk about the different places in your setting, how you move between them, and what activities happen in each area.

☺ Look at the different areas and decide if any of them could be moved outdoors. Plan a move of an area with the children and let them help to pack up and unpack.

Exploring time and place

1. Talk to the children about moving the role play area outside.
2. Discuss where it could go, how much space is needed, how every thing will be moved and who will do it.
3. You will need to consider:

   - 'Surveying the site' for a new home outdoors.
   - How each person will help and what they will do.
   - When the move will happen.
   - How things will be packed to keep them safe.
   - How everything will be transported.
   - Recreating the role play area in its new location.

4. Collect some packing materials: boxes, tape, string, bubble wrap, tissue, newspaper, dust sheets etc.
5. Try constructing or adapting a wheeled vehicle to carry the equipment – or you could adapt the bikes into removal vans and trailers.
5. Encourage the children to solve problems of access, safety, lifting and moving bulky loads and protecting fragile items.
6. Moving house will help you to develop children's problem solving skills and foster co operation, negotiation and teamwork.

And another idea......

* The older children could make a map to show the removal team where to move the role play area to.
* Play a removal game where children give each other verbal directions to follow.
* Put a big table outside and offer children experience of packing all sorts of items to keep them safe.

Building a house
Theme: Where I live

'Building a house' focuses on the sequence of events involved in constructing a building.

Making connections

'Building a house' could link with
'Our house',
'Places I like',
'Moving house',
and with topics on
Houses and homes,
Materials.

Key words

* build
* tools
* block
* brick
* plank
* wood
* plastic
* pipe
* stage
* plan
* cement
* walls

Getting started

☺ Gather together a wide range of different materials for construction. These could include construction sets, large and small wooden blocks, sand, clay, boxes and cartons, bricks, planks of wood, plastic piping and guttering, fabric.

☺ Provide lots of opportunities for the children to investigate them.

☺ Provide books and pictures showing the different stages in constructing a building.

☺ If you have some building work going on in the setting or nearby, you could take the children to watch building in action.

☺ If a family member works in the construction industry invite them in to talk to the children about the job they do.

☺ Remember health and safety guidance when working on large scale constructions. Negotiate safety rules with the children.

Exploring time and place

1. The outdoors is a great place for construction activities, with more space to build on a bigger scale, over a longer period of time.

2. When they have had plenty of free play building, help the children to plan a large scale construction outside. Use open questions and discussion to help them plan the different stages of the process:
   - What are we going to build? What will it look like?
   - Who is it for? How long will it take?
   - How big will it be? Where will we build it?
   - What materials will we need?
   - Where will we get these from?

3. Spend time on this planning stage to provide lots of opportunities for children to think through their ideas, express them in drawings and pictures, and organise the resources and help they need.

4. As they are constructing use every opportunity to draw attention to the different stages in the construction process and help the children to refer back to their original plans and ideas.

5. Record the whole design and construction process with a camera to capture all the different stages. Talk about any changes which were made to the original ideas.

And another idea......

* At a later date revisit the pictorial record of the construction project to help the children review and remember what they did.

* Use a collection of old tools to compare tools now and then .

* Make some sand and water 'cement' and practice sticking bricks together. Try using some real bricks.

In our street
Theme: Where I live

'In our street' focuses on looking for and looking at signs, street furniture and environmental print.

Making connections

'In our street' could link with 'Our house', 'Moving house' 'Going shopping' 'A day out' and with topics on Where we live, Communication.

Key words	* street * sign * name	* road * lane * direction	* traffic light * zebra crossing * post box	* light * stop * go

Getting started

☺ Share with the children a range of pictures and books showing street scenes. Include a range of different images – busy towns, city centres, small villages and country lanes. Talk about the different types of signs and writing in each location, including:

- ⓘ road signs and markings
- ⓘ directions
- ⓘ parking signs
- ⓘ street names
- ⓘ shop names
- ⓘ notices and adverts

☺ Look for examples of street furniture:

- ⓘ street lamps
- ⓘ post boxes
- ⓘ bus stops
- ⓘ seats
- ⓘ crossing signs
- ⓘ traffic lights
- ⓘ litter bins and recycling bins
- ⓘ hanging baskets
- ⓘ bus shelters
- ⓘ neon signs

Exploring time and place

1. Take the children on a walk in your neighbourhood. Ask them to look out for signs and street furniture.
2. Take time during the walk to talk about the signs and what they mean.
3. Look at where the different sorts of street furniture are and what they are for.
4. Take photographs of all the different types you see.
5. Back in your setting, talk to the children about where signs and street furniture could be introduced, especially out of doors. Decide where to put them so they would help people to:

   ? find their way around,

   ? move and play safely

   ? know where things are kept

   ? look after the environment.

6. Help the children to design and make some road signs to be used out of doors, for pedestrians and for wheeled toy drivers!
7. Look at different ways of improving the environment by introducing planters, litter bins and recycling points with their own signs.

And another idea......

* Invite your local road safety team into your setting.
* Use your photographs to remind the children of the signs they have seen.
* Put some small world street signs in the construction and brick areas.
* Put some card and markers in your writing area so children can make their own labels and notices.

Going shopping
Theme: Journeys

'Going shopping' is about observing and identifying features in the natural and built environment.

Making connections

'Going shopping' could link with
'What we like to eat',
'In our street',
'Where shall we go?',
and to topics on
Our Neighbourhood,
Food.

Key words	* I-spy * journey * shop	* road * street * sign	* map * plan * near	* far * next * turn

Getting started

☺ You could use 'What we like to eat' as a starting point to plan a journey in your local neighbourhood with a specific purpose in mind. You could plan to:
- look at environmental features, rural or urban,
- talk about and experience different methods of transport
- follow directions
- observe signs and environmental print.

☺ Talk to the children about the different journeys they make with their families. Don't forget that there will be some children who rarely leave their immediate neighbourhood whilst others will have experienced travelling abroad.

☺ Have some large scale maps and plans (or even aerial photos) of your neighbourhood available for the children to look at.

Exploring time and place

1. Some children will already be familiar with maps – they may have used them in your setting or at home. Others may have a natural interest in places and plans.
2. Talk with the children about a trip to the local shops. let them tell you how to get there, what you pass, and what you will find when you get there.
3. Use your knowledge of the children to work with a small group of 3 or 4 children to make an 'I-spy' book of the way to the shops, for everyone to use.
4. Take these children on the journey first. They will need a camera, (a digital camera will be best for making the 'I-spy' book). Children could also take clipboards, and pencils or felt pens. You will need a clipboard too, so you can record for younger or less confident children.
5. Encourage the children to record points of particular interest on the journey - signs, shops, street names, interesting windows and doors, fences and walls, trees, street furniture. Include some small details, numbers and symbols to encourage careful looking.
1. When you get back, work with the children to put the clues in order, so other children can use the book. Stick the clues in a scapbook or photo album. Then take other groups on the same trail.

And another idea......

* Play lots of 'I-spy' games!
* Help the children to produce a pictorial map of their journey.
* Introduce aspects of 'Healthy Living' by talking about making journeys on foot, rather than by car.
* Make some more 'I-spy' books to encourage the children to observe and recognise different features in the environment.

A day out
Theme: Journeys

'A day out' will provide opportunities for children to imagine a journey a long time ago.

Making connections

'A day out' could link with
'Things we use',
'Games and rhymes',
'On Holiday',
and topics on
The Victorians,
Journeys, Holidays.

Key words

* trip
* outing
* steam

* train
* charabanc
* coach

* cart
* travel
* seaside

* picnic
* deckchair
* picnic

Getting started

☺ Find a large, old suitcase. Pack a selection of items which would have been used in Victorian or Edwardian times.

☺ You could include:
>   mob-cap or bonnet; pinafore
>   waistcoat, cap
>   parasol, postcards or pictures

☺ Leave the suitcase in the role play area for the children to discover. You could use the contents of the suitcase to stimulate a discussion about life a long time ago - talking about similarities and differences.

☺ Equip the role play area with clothes and artefacts which the children can use to recreate 'a day out from the past'.

Exploring time and place

Younger children find it difficult to understand the concepts of 'long ago', but dressing up and being someone different is a good starter, and they really enjoy it!

1. Postcards, posters and books from the past can all provide starting points for talking about journeys and outings.
2. Talk to the children about how people travelled in the past- on foot, by horse and cart, on cycles, in steam trains and in charabancs. Your local museum or library may have resources which you can borrow to give a visual picture.
3. 'A day out' will provide the opportunity to take role play and construction outdoors. Help the children to design and make a bus or train using chairs, large blocks, boxes, wheels etc. The bikes could be converted into ice cream vendors (talk about how the ice-cream was kept cold) and about veteran cars! Look at some books to see what they looked like.
4. You may like to provide a picnic basket, metal buckets and spades and perhaps a deckchair or two (mind their fingers!).
5. Encourage the children to talk about the differences between outings in the past and now. Don't forget the ring games you could play. Or make a hopscotch or play simple cricket.

And another idea......

*   The children could make their own postcards to send to their families and friends.
*   Enjoy songs such as 'Daisy, Daisy' and 'I Do Like to Be Beside the Seaside'.
*   Look at photos of parents and grandparents at the beach or on holiday, and talk about the differences

On holiday
Theme: Journeys

'On holiday' provides opportunities to find out about places near and far away.

Making connections

'A day out' could link with 'Things we use', 'Games and rhymes', 'On Holiday', and topics on The Victorians, Journeys, Holidays.

Key words
- holiday
- travel
- book
- form
- hot
- cold
- winter
- summer
- pack
- ticket
- suitcase
- money

Getting started

☺ Collect a selection of brochures and posters from your local travel agent. Try to include winter and summer, city and country, abroad and at home.

☺ Use these to turn your role play or mark making area in to a Travel Agency. Include:
- ✎ Telephone and computer
- ✎ Booking forms and notebooks
- ✎ Globe, map of the world
- ✎ Timetables and tickets

☺ Talk about holidays and the different places which the children have visited. Remember to include day trips and shorter local visits. Some children may be able to show the others where they have been by using a map or a globe.

Exploring time and place

1. Encourage the children to use the Travel Agent communication area and to take on different roles. Model behaviour and help them to think about arranging holidays to:

    Different places;
    - hot or cold, sunny or snowy
    - across the sea, over the mountains, to the town
    - to the seaside, country or city.

    Different transport
    - by car
    - by train
    - by aeroplane
    - by boat

    and where we stay

    - in a tent
    - in a caravan or chalet
    - in a hotel, a flat or an apartment

2. In the role play area provide a range of different holiday clothes, accessories, bags and cases to pack, money to spend and postcards to write. The children can then decide where to 'Go on holiday'.

And another idea......

* Help each child to make a passport.
* Ask the children's families to send postcards to the setting when they are on holiday.
* Set up a holiday camp out doors – use 'pop up' tents and dens the children make.
* Have an outdoor café, or a beach, or a swimming pool, or a theme park!

What can we find?

Theme: Journeys

'What can we find?' is about looking at different habitats and the plants and animals that live there.

Making connections

'What can we find?' could link with
'On holiday',
'Where shall we go?'
and topics on
Water,
Plants,
Minibeasts.

Key words				
	* animal	* minibeast	* beach	* leaf, shell
	* plant	* garden	* park	* sand, stone
	* bird	* wood	* tree	* clay, soil

Getting started

☺ Arrange a visit to the local park, the beach or a wood or garden.

☺ Before you go look at books and pictures showing the environment you are going to visit. Talk to the children about the different plants and animals they might find there.

☺ Make sure the adults are familiar with the environment they are going to visit and they know and can name the range of plants, trees, birds and animals.

☺ Take some suitable reference books with you, as well as magnifiers, bug viewers, pond tray and nets. Take a Perry's Pooter if you have one.

☺ Collect suitable natural materials to bring back to the setting – stones, twigs, shells, driftwood, sand, leaves, seaweed etc.

☺ Talk to the children about conservation and respect for the natural environment.

Exploring time and place

1. Back in the setting gather all your 'treasure' together and encourage the children to talk about all the different things they found, and where they found them.

2. Provide the resources – good quality magnifiers and viewers - to enable the children to observe closely. Don't forget to talk about how things feel, what they sound like and what they smell of. Draw attention to the dangers of tasting things.

3. Use pictures and reference material to help the children identify the different things they have collected.

4. Choose a suitable area to recreate the habitat you visited using the natural materials you collected. This could be indoors or outdoors.

5. You could add models of minibeasts, sea creatures, plants or animals, depending on the sort of habitat you have visited.

6. Offer the children clay or dough to make their own minibeasts. When they are dry and painted, the children could make habitats for their creatures. Encourage children to look carefully and use reference books to check on shapes and colours.

REMEMBER! Never take living creatures out of their habitats unless you can maintain the features of that habitat AND return them within hours to the place where you found them.

And another idea......

* You might choose to visit another environment at a different time and make comparisons.

* Set up a wormery or ant farm so you can observe creatures in their natural environment.

* Put a few slugs or snails in an aquarium with some turf and some leaves to eat. Keep the turf damp and return the creatures after a couple of days.

Where shall we go?
Theme: Journeys

'Where shall we go?' combines aspects of many of the other activities in this book by looking at planning a journey.

Making connections

'Where shall we go?' could link with
'Moving House',
'In our Street',
'Going Shopping',
'On Holiday', 'A Day Out',
'What Can we Find?'.

Key words
* choose
* decide
* plan
* visit
* journey
* book
* phone
* letter
* ticket
* invitation
* cost
* time

Getting started

☺ Many of the activities in 'The Little Book of a Sense of Time and Place' involve planning visits – near and far. Some of these visits are imaginary and some are real.

☺ When organising any visit, use the opportunities to involve the children in

🚌 making choices and decisions,

🚌 planning, predicting, list making,

🚌 communicating.

☺ Planning a visit 'for real' gives a meaningful context for the children to practice skills and develop positive dispositions.

☺ 'Where shall we go?' can be used as a reference point for any visits which you make during the year.

Exploring time and place

1. Making choices and decisions

When you begin to plan a visit or journey include the children in discussions about where to go and what the purpose of the visit is. Involve them in the decisions and choices you make about where and when to go, how to get there and what to take. Don't forget that you will need to take notice of the suggestions and decisions the children make. This stage needs skills of negotiation and co-operation.

2. Planning, predicting, list making

Organising a visit will give children the experience of planning in a series of logical steps. Help them to think about the whole visit and then to break it down into different as aspects such as transport, supervision, cost, timing and Health and Safety. 'What will we need?' 'How will we carry it?' 'How will we keep safe?' etc. Remember that you will need to carry out a risk assessment for any visit.

3. Communicating

This is an opportunity to give children real experience of different ways of communicating - writing, speaking, asking questions, using the telephone and using the computer. Involve them in booking transport, paying for tickets and telling families about the visit.

And another idea......

* Encourage the children to use their organisational skills in other contexts such as role play and small world play.
* Trust a small group of children to organise an event within your setting, with adult support when needed, invited or requested.

Background Information
Nursery Rhymes and action songs

These action songs are both related to work in the past- the life of the farmer and the mill worker.

Oats and Beans

Oats and beans and barley grow,
Oats and beans and barley grow.
Do you or I or anyone know
How oats and beans and barley grow?

First the farmer sows his seed,
Then he stands and takes his ease.
He stamps his feet and claps his hands,
And turns around to view the land.
Oats and beans (repeat).

Waiting for a partner,
Waiting for a partner.
Open the gate and let her in
And greet her when she enters in.
Oats and beans (repeat).

Now you're married you must obey,
You must be true to all you say.
You must be kind, you must be good,
And help your wife to chop the wood.

Oats and beans and barley grow,
Oats and beans and barley grow.
Do you or I or anyone know
How oats and beans and barley grow?

Wind the Bobbin

Wind the bobbin up and
Wind the bobbin up and
   Pull, pull, clap, clap, clap.
Wind the bobbin up and
Wind the bobbin up and
   Pull, pull, clap, clap, clap.
Point to the ceiling, point to the floor,
Point to the window, point to the door.
Clap your hands together, one, two, three,
And put your hands upon your knee.

Hand gestures accompany the words - winding the bobbin first in one direction and then in the other.

Many nursery rhymes relate to places, people and customs of the past:

Ride a Cock Horse

Ride a cock horse
To Banbury Cross
To see a fine lady upon a white horse.
Rings on her fingers
And bells on her toes
She shall have music wherever she goes.

Wee Willie Winkie

Wee Willie Winkie
Runs through the town,
Upstairs and downstairs
In his nightgown.
Rapping at the windows,
Calling through the lock,
Are all the children in their beds?
It's past eight o'clock.

Sing a Song of Sixpence

Sing a song of sixpence,
A pocket full of rye,
Four and twenty blackbirds,
Baked in a pie.
When the pie was opened,
The birds began to sing.
Wasn't that a dainty dish
To set before the king?

The king was in his counting house,
Counting out his money.
The queen was in the parlour,
Eating bread and honey.
The maid was in the garden,
Hanging out the clothes,
When down came a blackbird
And pecked off her nose.
She made such a commotion,
That little Jenny Wren
Flew down into the garden,
And popped it on again.

Circle and dancing games

Some old circle and dancing games became popular among children after battles hundreds of years ago. One of these is:

The Grand Old Duke of York

The Grand Old Duke of York,
He had ten thousand men,
He marched them up to the top of the hill,
And he marched them down again.
And when they were up, they were up,
And when they were down, they were down,
And when they were only half way up,
They were neither up nor down.

The children find a partner. They form two lines with each pair facing one another. The pair of children at the front of the line join hands and side skip down between the facing lines and then back up to their position, while the other children clap and sing. The leading pair make an arch with their hands and the rest of the children join hands with their partners. Each pair goes through the arch, separates, turns and skips round the outside and back up the middle. The first pair join the end of the line after everyone has gone through the arch. The dancing game is repeated.

Nursery Rhymes and action songs

The Big Ship Sails

This dancing game retells a story from the time of canals, ships and seafaring.

1. The big ship sails on the Alley Alley O,
The Alley Alley O, the Alley Alley O.
The Alley Alley O, the Alley Alley O.
On the last day of September.

2. Mother, mother, mother may I go?
Mother may I go? Mother may I go?
Mother, mother, mother may I go
On the last day of September?

3. Yes my daughter, you may go,
You may go, you may go.
Yes my daughter you may go
On the last day of September.

4. The Captain said, 'It will never, never do,
Never, never do; never, never do'.
The Captain said, 'It will never, never do'
On the last day of September.

5. The big ship sank to the bottom of the sea,
The bottom of the sea, the bottom of the sea.
The big ship sank to the bottom of the sea
On the last day of September.

6. We all dip our heads in the deep blue sea,
The deep blue sea, the deep blue sea.
The deep blue sea, the deep blue sea.
On the last day of September.

To play this game the children join hands in a long line. The child at the front of the line puts their hand firmly against a wall to make an arch.
The child at the back of the line leads the children through the arch until all the children are through. The first child now has his arms crossed. The leader then takes the line of children under an arch created by the first and second children. This continues until all of the children have their arms crossed. Sing the first three verses while you do this!

Now join the line into a circle -the first and last children join hands, stil with arms crossed. Shake heads during the fourth verse, bend the knees and rise again during the fifth verse and bend heads towards the ground during the last verse.
For younger children, just sing the song with the actions!

Oranges and Lemons

is both historic and includes the names of churches in London.
Two children join hands to make an arch. One is 'orange' and one is 'lemon'.
The other children form a line behind each other, holding on to the waist of the child in front. They sing the song as they walk through the arch, round and through again.

On the last line of the song the arch comes down and catches a child. The child chooses to be an orange or a lemon and joins on behind the appropriate side of the arch, holding the waist of the child in front. The song begins again.

Oranges and lemons',
Say the bells of St.Clements,
'I owe you five farthings',
Say the bells of St. Martins.
'When will you pay me?',
Say the bells of Old Bailey.
'When I grow rich',
Say the bells of Shoreditch.
'When will that be?',
Says the bells of Stepney.
'I do not know,'
Says the great bell of Bow.
Here comes a candle
To light you to bed.
And here comes a chopper
To chop off your head!

Ring a Roses

Ring a Roses is a traditional circle game dating back to the time of the plague when posies were hung outside doors to ward off disease.

Ring a ring a roses
(Dance in a circle)
A pocket full of posies,
(Dance in a circle)
Atishoo, atishoo,
(Mime sneezing)
We all fall down
(Fall down to the ground).

OR

The cows are in the meadow
(Lying still on the ground)
Lying fast asleep
(Pretend to sleep)
Atishoo, atishoo,
(Mime sneezing)
We all get up again.
(Jump up again)

Here are some more variations (you will have to make up your own movements!):

The King has sent his daughter,
To fetch a pail of water,
Atishoo, atishoo,
We all fall down.

OR for swimmers

Ring a ring a roses
Water up our noses,
Atishoo, atishoo,
But we won't drown!

OR

The cows are in the meadow,
Eating buttercups,
Atishoo, atishoo,
We all jump up.

OR

Fishes in the water,
Fishes in the sea,
We all jump up
With a one, two, three.

and finally, an Irish version

Daddy's in the milk jug,
Mummy's in the cup,
Baby's in the sugar bowl,
We all jump up!

Variations are from "This Little Puffin"

The Muffin Man

The Muffin Man would have been a familiar sight in towns and cities, selling his muffins from a tray hung round his neck. Buy some muffins from a bakers or supermarket and sing this song while you eat them. Or dance as you sing in pairs or a group.

Do you know the muffin man?
The muffin man, the muffin man.
Do you know the muffin man
Who lives in Drury Lane-O?
The partner responds, with arms folded, skipping on the spot.

Yes I know the muffin man,
The muffin man, the muffin man.
Yes I know the muffin man
Who lives in Drury Lane-O
These two children then stand opposite two others and the game is repeated until all children have responded. Then they sing altogether.

We all know the muffin man,
The muffin man, the muffin man.
We all know the muffin man
Who lives in Drury Lane-O
Carry on till all the children are dancing.

Web Sites and Resources

English Heritage   www.english-heritage.org.uk
Produce free resources which can be downloaded from their site – a useful
background resource for staff. Contact English Heritage sites in your local area
to discuss educational visits.

National Trust   www.nationaltrust.org.uk
Information on National Trust properties and events in your area. The learning
and discovery site features the adventures of Trusty the hedgehog.

The National Virtual Museum   www.24hourmuseum.org.uk
Information about museums and events in your area, plus a teacher's information
page with downloadable resources. Details of exhibits, loan collections and
workshops provided by museums and historical associations across the country.

www.show.me.uk
Children's museum information and events.

The Geographical Association   www.geography.org.uk
This website has an early years and primary section with lists of resources including:
  Geography starts here.   Angela M. Milner 1996
  Geography through play.   Angela M. Milner 1997

The Historical Association   www.history.org.uk
Key Stage 1 education resources and publications.

Construction Industry Training Board (CITB)   www.citb.org.uk
Produces education resources for Key Stage 1 as part of its Construction
Industry Awards Scheme (ccas).

Learning through Landscapes   www.ltl.org.uk
Provides information and advice on using and improving outdoor areas and
promoting outdoor play. Has a dedicated early years site and is actively promoting
the involvement of early years practitioners.

Royal Mail   www.royalmailgroup.com
Runs an education scheme of 'Royal Mail volunteers' and has produced a Key
Stage 1 resource entitled Lenny the letter.

Web Sites and Resources
(Continued)

Past Times Historical Gifts   www.pasttimes.com
Reproduction artefacts from the past.

Articles of Faith   www.articlesoffaith.co.uk
Historical and multicultural resources and books.

Access to farms   www.farmsforteachers.org.uk
The website lists farms across the country which host educational visits, including facilities provided and age groups catered for.

Three Bears Playthings Steward House, High Street, Rothbury. NE65 7TL.
Tel: 01669 620315
Role play costumes and equipment to help re create different scenarios & locations.

Reflections on Learning and Commotion Group   www.commotiongroup.co.uk
www.reflectionsonlearning.co.uk
Produce communication boxes and mirrors, magnifiers, hand lenses, Perry's pooters, pond tray and nets, wormerys, ant farms, habitat and life cycle books and posters.

Books

You may find the following books useful as starting points and for creating the context for the activities suggested in this book. Remember you may be able to borrow these from the children's section of your local library.

Building, homes and moving house

Kipper	Mick Inkpen	Hodder
Kipper's Tree House	Mick Inkpen	Hodder
Builder for a day	Pop up book	Dorling Kindersley
Bob's big story collection		BBC Publications
Nothing	Mick Inkpen	Hodder Books
The Berenstain Bear's Moving Day	Stan and Jan Berenstain	Chronicle Books
Little Miss Trouble moving house	Roger Hargreaves	Egremont
Moving House – Usborne First Experiences		Usborne
Cleo on the move	Stella Blackstone	Barefoot Books
Boomer's big day	Constance McGeorge	Chronicle Books

Journeys and visits

Katie in London	James Mayhew	Orchard Books
Mr Gumpy's outing	John Burningham	Red Fox
Mog at the zoo	Helen Nicholl	Puffin
The shopping basket	John Burningham	Red Fox
The train ride	June Crebbin	Walker Books
Going on a plane	First experiences	Usborne

Different times and places

Out and about through the year	Shirley Hughes	Walker Books
Rhymes for Annie Rose	Shirley Hughes	Walker Books
We're going on a bear hunt	Michael Rosen	Walker Books
Where is Maisy going?	Lucy Cousins	Walker Books
Handa's surprise	Eileen Browne	Walker Books
Katie Morag delivers the mail	Mairi Hedderwick	Red Fox
Peepo	Allen and Janet Ahlberg	Penguin
The big Milly Molly Mandy Storybook, Joyce Lancaster Brisley		Kingfisher
Old Bear	Jane Hissey	Random House

Books (Continued)

Times of the day and the year, routines

Cat on the hill	Michael Foreman	Andersen Press
And the good brown earth	Kathy Henderson	Walker Books
My grandmother's clock	Geraldine McCaughrean	Collins
Fidget and Quilley, Are you ready?	Mike Hanes	Hodder
Fidget and Quilley Countdown to bedtime;	Mike Hanes	Hodder
Starting school	Janet and Allen Ahlberg	Puffin

Urban buildings and signs

I-spy in the town	Michelin publications

See also

The Little Book of Nursery Rhymes	Featherstone Education
The Little Book of Maths Songs and Games	Featherstone Education
The Little Book of Persona Dolls	Featherstone Education

If you have found this book useful you might also like ...

**The Little Book of
Investigations**
LB20
ISBN 1-904187-66-8

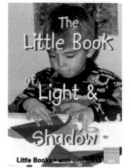

**The Little Book of
Light & Shadow**
LB25
ISBN 1-904187-81-1

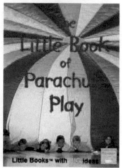

**The Little Book of
Parachute Play**
LB24
ISBN 1-904187-80-3

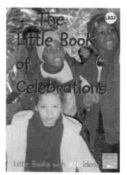

**The Little Book of
Celebrations**
LB32
ISBN 1-904187-59-5

All available from

Featherstone Education   PO Box 6350

Lutterworth   LE17 6ZA

T:0185 888 1212   F:0185 888 1360

on our web site

www.featherstone.uk.com

and from selected
book suppliers